W9-AUY-136

Easy Origami

Didier Boursin

FIREFLY BOOKS

ONSLOW COUNTY PUBLIC LIBRARY
58 DORIS AVENUE EAST
JACKSONVILLE, NC 28540

A FIREFLY BOOK

Published by Firefly Books Ltd. 2005

Copyright © Desain & Tolra/VUEF 2004

Original title: Pilages et decoupages faciles, Larousse, Paris

All rights reserved. No part of this publication may be reproduced, stored in a retrieval system, or transmitted in any form or by any means, electronic, mechanical, photocopying, recording or otherwise, without the prior written permission of the Publisher.

First printing

Also available from Firefly Books
Origami Paper Airplanes
Origami Paper Animals
Advanced Origami

Publisher Cataloging-in-Publication Data (U.S.)

Boursin, Didier.
    Easy origami / Didier Boursin.
Originally published as Pliages et découpages faciles ; France : Dessain et Tolra, 2002.
[64] p. : col. ill., photos. ; cm.
Summary: Various origami designs ranging in skill levels.
ISBN 1-55297-928-8   ISBN 1-55297-939-3 (pbk.)
1. Origami. 1. Title.
736/.982 22 TT870.B687 2005

National Library of Canada Cataloguing in Publication

Boursin, Didier
    Easy origami / Didier Boursin.
Translation of: Pliages et découpages faciles.
ISBN 1-55297-928-8 (bound).—ISBN 1-55297-939-3 (pbk.)
    1. Origami. 1. Title.
TT870.B68513 2005   736'.982
C2004-905985-8

Published in the United States by
Firefly Books (U.S.) Inc.
P.O. Box 1338, Ellicott Station
Buffalo, New York 14205

Published in Canada by
Firefly Books Ltd.
66 Leek Crescent
Richmond Hill, Ontario L4B 1H1

Design: Didier Boursin
Photography: Cactus Studio
Translation and origami consultation: John Reid

The publisher gratefully acknowledges the financial support for our publishing program by the Canada Council for the Arts, the Ontario Arts Council and the Government of Canada through the Book Publishing Industry Development Program.

Printed in Singapore

Acknowledgments
I would like to thank all those who helped me in the creation of this book, including my children and especially Nina, who contributed enthusiastically to the photographs. I would also like to thank everyone I met at my demonstrations and exhibitions who appreciated my work. I would like to thank the entire editorial team, especially Catherine Franck and Valérie Gendreau. I am grateful to Fabrice Besse, who photographed my models with patience, and to Setsuko, whose advice and good nature are always appreciated.

You may send your comments to me at:
Didier Boursin
17, rue Sainte-Croix-de-la-Bretonnerie, 75004 Paris
www.origami-creation.com

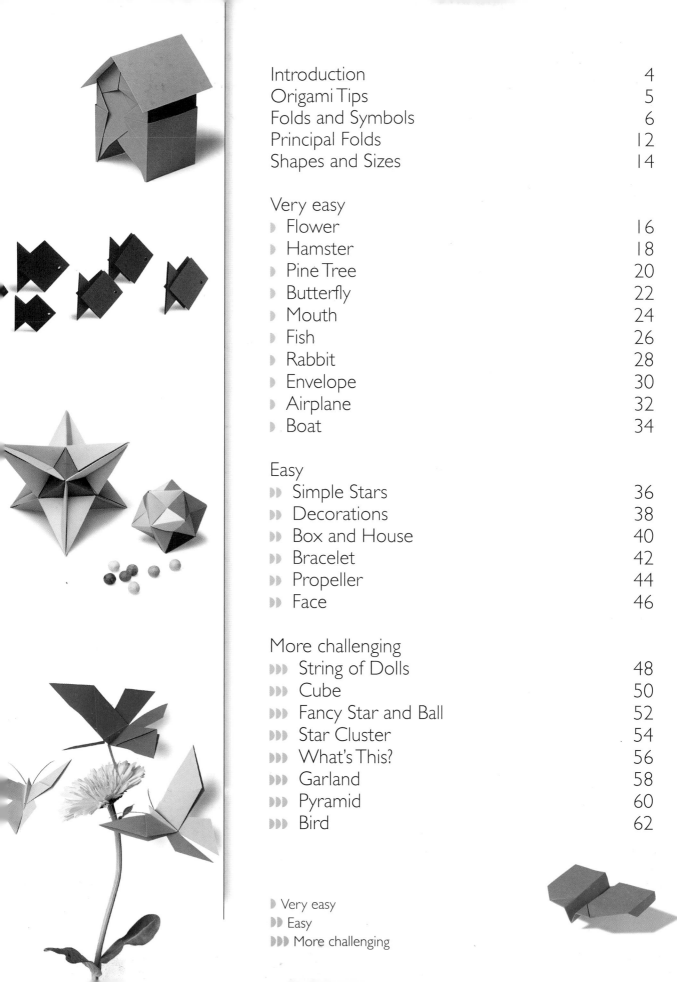

▶ Very easy
▶▶ Easy
▶▶▶ More challenging

Introduction

Creating a book of paper folds takes time — and lots of it. I often hear the comment, "All you have to do is think." Few people understand that it sometimes takes several months to adjust a model and its step-by-step instructions.

Creating a very simple fold is actually quite complicated because I try to use a minimum of material for maximum expression. For each model, I invite you to appreciate the subtleties of its construction, its beauty and its gracefulness.

For many years, I have tried to change origami, including the overall concept about it. It is an ephemeral art form, a means of reflection and poetic expression. By its nature, it is suitable for children and enthusiasts of all ages. It will also interest teachers, who can use it in a lighthearted yet practical manner to teach the sometimes complex concepts of geometry.

Each model is an addition to one's collection of games or gallery of paintings and drawings. I hope this book stimulates curiosity and imagination, develops creativity, and brings a little happiness to every day.

Didier Boursin

Origami Tips

First of all, make yourself comfortable at a table, alone or with some friends. Start folding calmly, without getting discouraged if the fold seems difficult at first. With a little thought and focus, you will have the satisfaction of making a model with your own hands. Eventually, you'll be able to fold effortlessly — practically with your eyes shut.

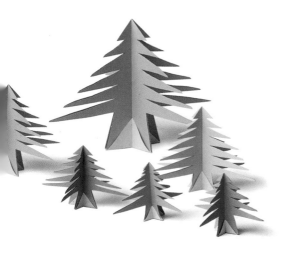

The Paper

Choose white or colored paper, like photocopy paper, to start. Avoid drawing paper (too thick), tracing paper (too brittle) and newsprint (too soft). Once you have experience making the model, you can move on to better paper or a larger size.

The Shape

The required paper shape is indicated at the beginning of each model: square, A4 (see page 14), 8 1/2 x 11, or very small. For a model made up of several pieces, use small sheets (3–4 in./8–10 cm) or one-quarter of an A4 or 8 1/2 x 11 sheet. For a one-piece model, use a larger square (8–10 in./20–30 cm) or a full A4 or 8 1/2 x 11 sheet.

Pages 14–15 cover size and shape. They explain how to make a square from a rectangle, a rectangle from a square, and other shapes.

Levels of Difficulty

The models are presented at three levels of difficulty. I suggest that you begin with the easiest. Before starting, read pages 6–11, which explain the symbols, the folds and the bases used in this book. Pages 12–13 show in detail the principal folds of each model. The easy folds are at the bottom and the more complex ones are at the top.

Folds and Symbols

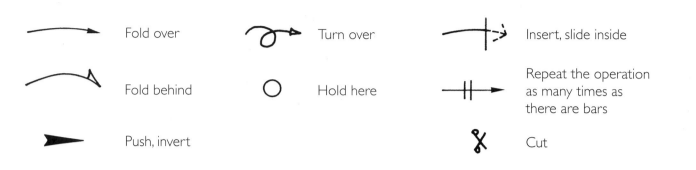 Fold over   Turn over   Insert, slide inside

Fold behind   Hold here   Repeat the operation as many times as there are bars

Push, invert   Cut

Valley Fold

Fold a square of paper up in half.

You have a valley fold.

Mountain Fold

 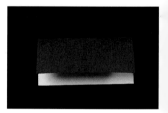

Fold a square of paper in half behind.

You have a mountain fold.

Crease

Carefully note the difference between folding the paper and creasing the paper. In the first case you keep the fold; in the second case you fold it, then unfold it.

Cut

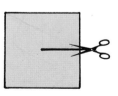

Cut along the line.

Join the Points

Fold one point to the spot indicated.

Flatten the fold.

Preliminary Base

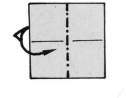

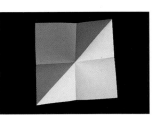
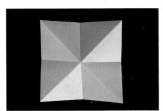

Mountain crease a square on the median …

… then mountain crease the second median.

Valley crease the diagonal …

… then valley crease the second diagonal.

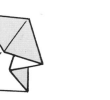

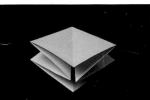

Press the center from behind.

Hold two opposite sides and join the folds to form a small square.

Flatten.

You have a preliminary base.

Waterbomb Base

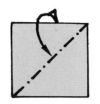 

 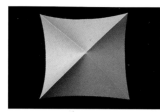 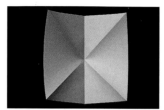 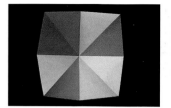

Mountain crease the diagonal of a square of paper …

… then crease the other diagonal.

Valley crease the square in half …

… then valley crease in half in the other direction.

 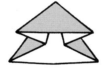 

Press in the center from behind.

Hold two opposite corners and join the folds to form a triangle, then flatten the whole model.

You have a waterbomb base.

Squash Fold

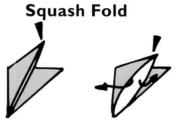 

Raise to vertical.

Press and … open.

Flatten.

Inside Reverse Fold

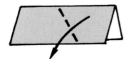 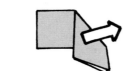  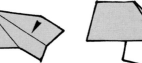

Fold a square in half and valley crease downward.

Then open.

Make the center crease a valley on the right side. The other three sides should have mountain folds. Close the left side.

You have an inside reverse fold.

Outside Reverse Fold

 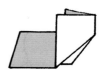

This drawing shows how to make an outside reverse fold.

Fold a square in half and valley crease upward.

Then open.

Mountain crease the angled folds and the center fold on the right side. Close the right side.

You have an outside reverse fold.

Bird Base

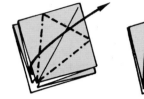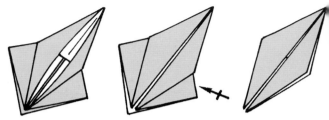

Start with a preliminary base and fold the edges to the center crease.

Fold down the upper triangle.

After unfolding the three points, hold the bottom point of the top layer.

Bring the point up along its folds.

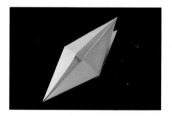

Flatten everything.

Turn over and repeat the same steps, folding the side and then the triangle.

After unfolding the sides, stretch out the point along its folds.

You have a bird base.

Rabbit Ear Fold

Fold the side.

Unfold.

Fold the other side.

Unfold.

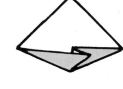

Fold up the two sides
while pinching the point.

Flatten …

… like this.

Principal Folds

Here you can see at a glance the different techniques needed to complete the folds in this book. Note that the folds get more elaborate as you move upward from the bottom of the page.

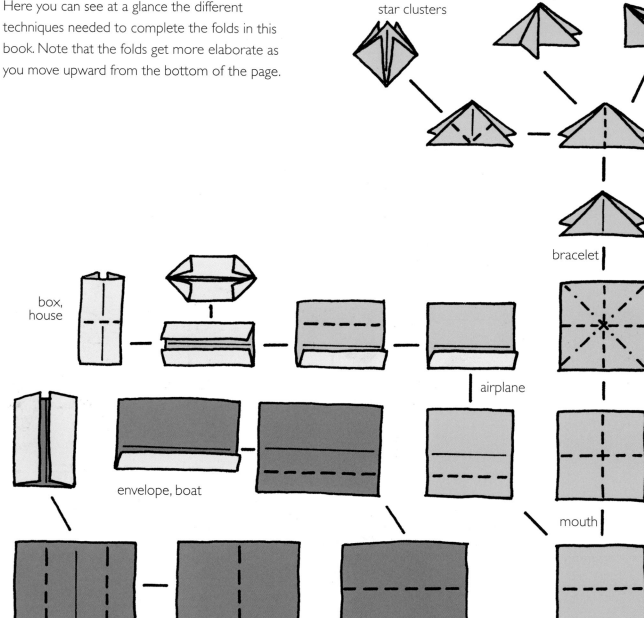

star clusters

fancy stars

pine tree, decoration

bracelet

box, house

airplane

envelope, boat

mouth

cube, ball, string of dolls

simple stars

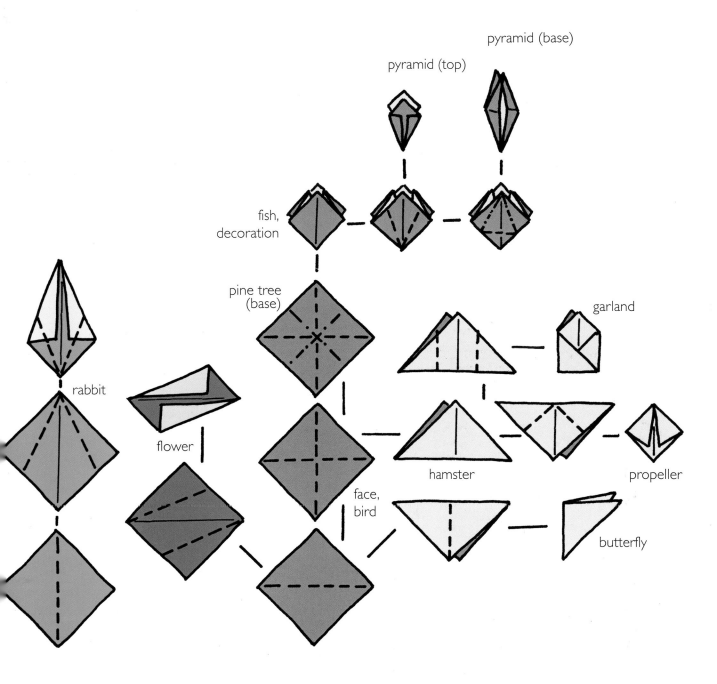

pyramid (base)

pyramid (top)

fish,
decoration

pine tree
(base)

garland

rabbit

flower

hamster

propeller

face,
bird

butterfly

Shapes and Sizes

You'll find all the information here that you need to make squares and "A4" sheets. Once you're familiar with the shapes, try placing pieces alongside one another to make other shapes. Or cut the squares along fold lines and rearrange the pieces to make new designs.

Hint: You may purchase square Origami paper or cut your own squares from a sheet of letter-sized or A4 paper. Origami instructions often refer to A4 paper. An A4 sheet can be made by trimming ⅝ in./1.5 cm from the width of a letter-sized sheet.

rectangle

square

square

equilateral triangle

right-angled triangle

vertical   horizontal   diagonal

From Rectangle to Square

Cross two A4 or 8½ x 11 sheets to get a square.

Fold the wide edge to the long edge.

Cut off.

From Square to Rectangle

Fold one side.   Cut off.

A4 Size

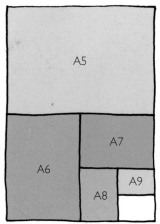

By dividing an A4 sheet you get A5, A6, A7 ...

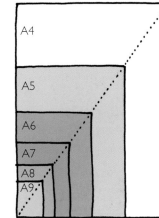

These sizes can be aligned on their diagonals.

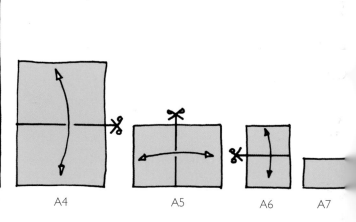

A4   A5   A6   A7

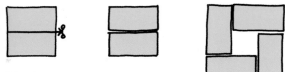

Cut in two.

  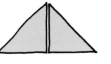 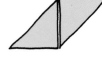 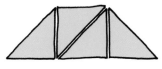

Cut in two. square triangle parallelogram trapezium

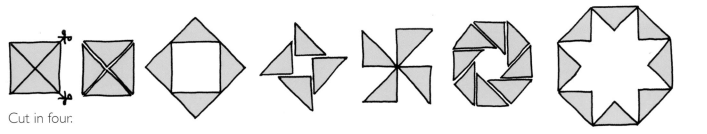

Cut in four.

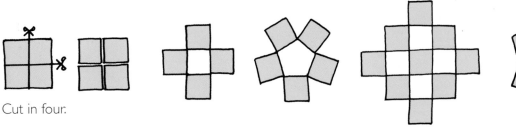 

Cut in four.

Cut in four.

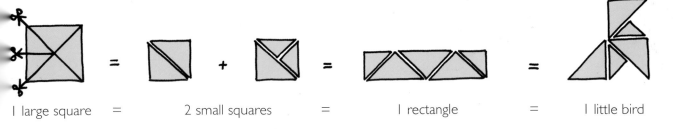

I large square = 2 small squares = I rectangle = I little bird

15

Flower

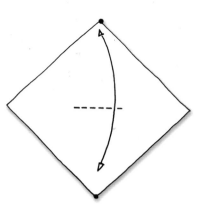

1 Fold in half, marking only the center, then unfold.

◗ **Very easy**

Pick papers of all colors: this way you can make a magnificent garden or a beautiful bouquet with an intoxicating fragrance.

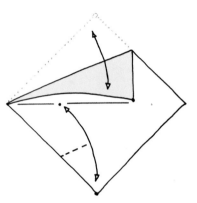

2 Fold the sides along the center crease, marking just the edges.

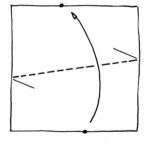

3 Fold up, connecting the edge marks.

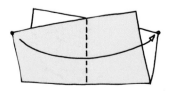

4 Fold in half, connecting the points.

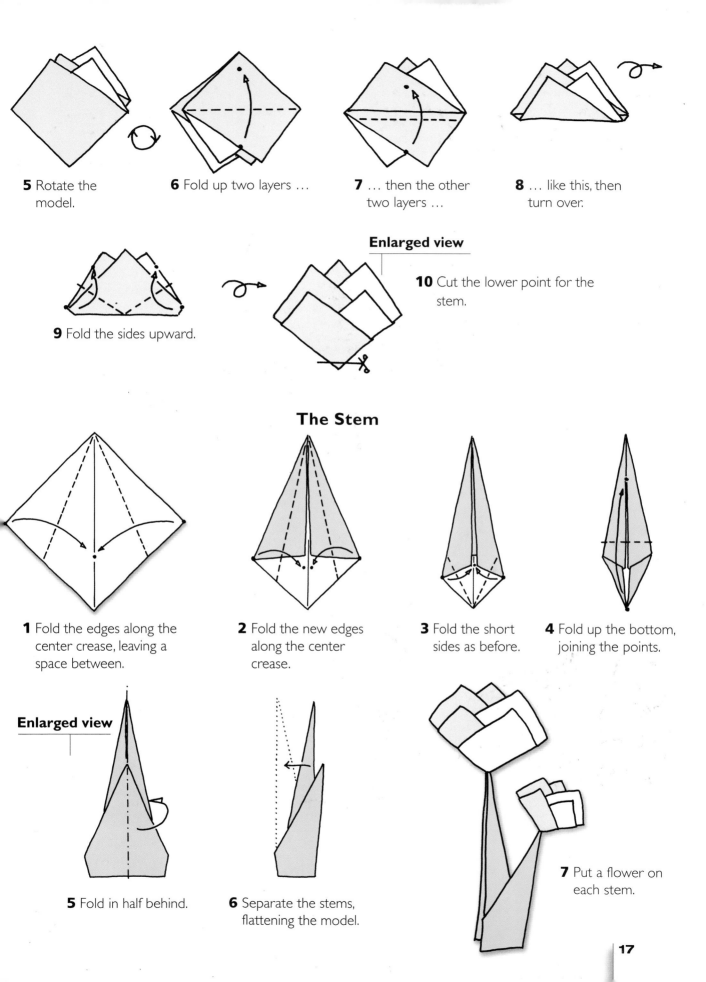

5 Rotate the model.

6 Fold up two layers …

7 … then the other two layers …

8 … like this, then turn over.

9 Fold the sides upward.

Enlarged view

10 Cut the lower point for the stem.

The Stem

1 Fold the edges along the center crease, leaving a space between.

2 Fold the new edges along the center crease.

3 Fold the short sides as before.

4 Fold up the bottom, joining the points.

Enlarged view

5 Fold in half behind.

6 Separate the stems, flattening the model.

7 Put a flower on each stem.

Hamster

▶ **Very easy**

These little rodents are an affectionate and mischievous bunch. Have fun making several hamsters, and give each one a funny name.

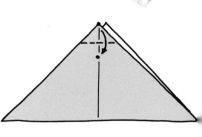

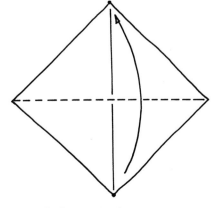

1 Crease the middle of a square.

2 Fold in half, joining the points.

3 Fold the upper triangle down to make the ears.

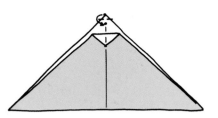

4 Fold another small triangle to form the nose …

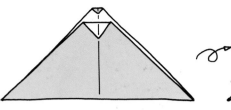

5 … like this, then turn it over.

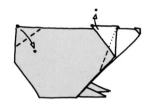

6 Fold the points toward the outside to make the feet.

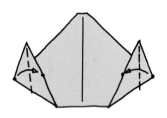

7 Narrow the feet by folding in half.

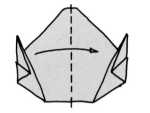

8 Fold everything in half.

9 Pull up the ears, then flatten the new fold.

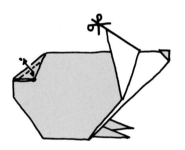

10 Separate the ears with a scissor cut. For the tail, make a pleat fold at the back.

Details of the pleat fold

11a Unfold.

11b Make an inside reverse fold (see page 9) …

Details

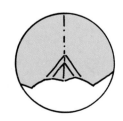

11c … open fold slightly …

11d … then fold out the small triangle for the appearance of a tail.

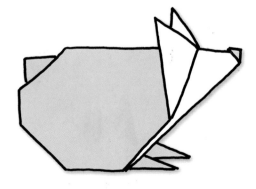

12 And you have a hamster.

Pine Tree

▶ **Very easy**

These pine trees are magnificent. If you create a forest, you can decorate the whole house. Hang them up or set them on a table for a lovely effect.

The Trunk and Branches

1 Fold a waterbomb base (see page 8) from a square piece of paper.

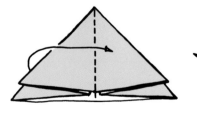

2 Fold everything in half.

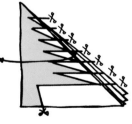

3 To create the branches, cut longer and longer notches, leaving space for the trunk. Open up to get two sets of branches on each side.

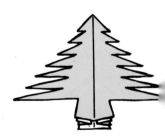

4 You can stop here and glue the parts o the trunk together. Or continue and make the base of the tree.

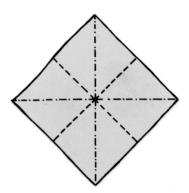

The Base

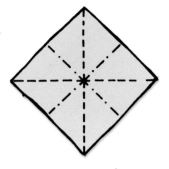

1 Fold a preliminary base (see page 7) with a square one-third the size used for the trunk, then unfold.

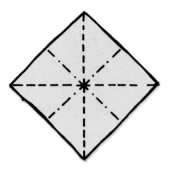

2 Make creases by folding the four corners to the center, then refold the preliminary base.

Assembly

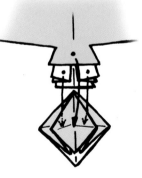

1 Place the trunk between the layers of the base as far as the crease.

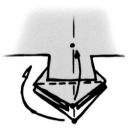

2 Fold up the triangles in front and back.

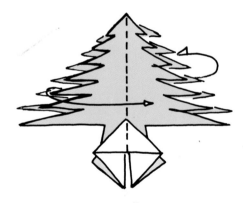

3 Fold one layer in front to the right and one in back to the left, and fold up the remaining triangles.

4 You can make trees of different sizes.

Butterfly

▶ **Very easy**

Fold butterflies in all sizes and colors and hang them all over your room. You can also glue them to birthday cards and party invitations.

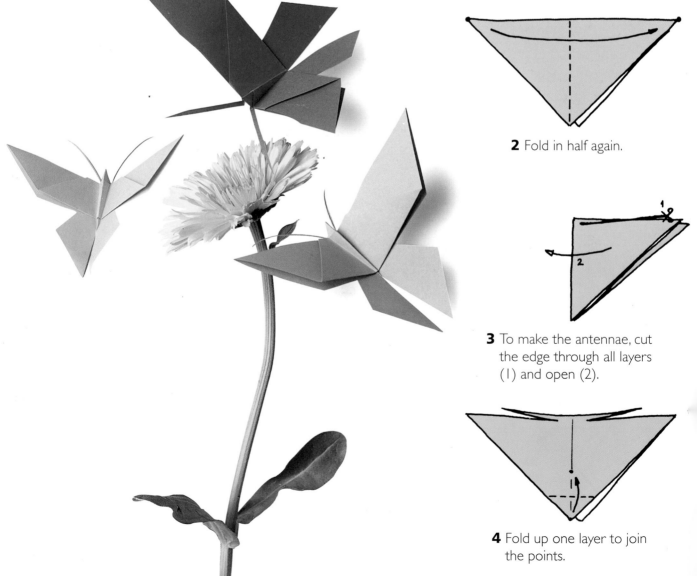

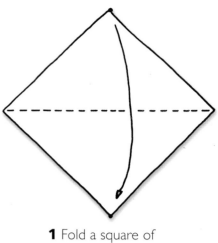

1 Fold a square of paper in half.

2 Fold in half again.

3 To make the antennae, cut the edge through all layers (1) and open (2).

4 Fold up one layer to join the points.

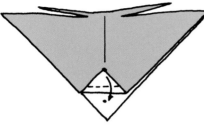

5 Make a pleat by folding the triangle down.

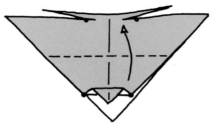

6 Fold up, joining the points.

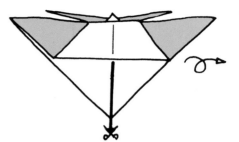

7 Cut on the heavy line, then turn it over.

8 Fold in half.

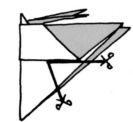

9 Cut through all the layers along the heavy lines.

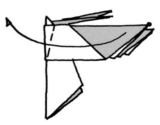

10 Fold the top wing on an angle …

11 … like this, then turn over.

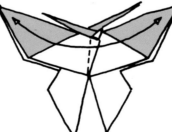

12 Fold the other wing, joining the points.

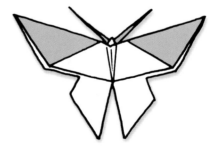

13 Open your butterfly and pull the antennae up.

Mouth

▶ **Very easy**

Draw eyes and a nose on this character ___ ause
your friends. You can provide the voice a___ move
the mouth.

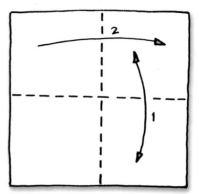

1 Crease the horizontal center of a square (1), then fold it in half to the right (2).

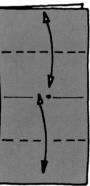

2 Crease by folding the ends to the center crease.

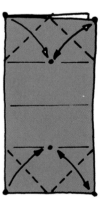

3 Fold the four corners, then unfold the corners on the right side.

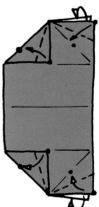

4 On the left side, fold the upper and lower corners back along the folded edge. On the right side, fold the top layer along the crease, then repeat behind.

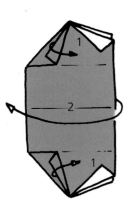

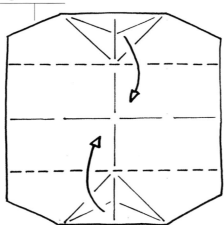

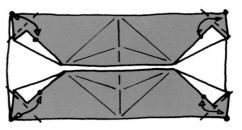

5 Unfold the corners on the left (1) and open up (2).

6 Refold the sides along the center crease.

7 Crease the four corners along the upper layer.

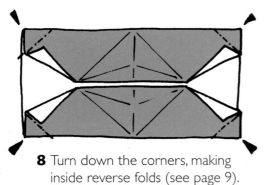

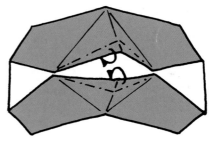

8 Turn down the corners, making inside reverse folds (see page 9).

9 To lock the sides, reverse the flaps, folding them inside under all the layers.

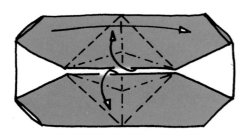

10 To shape the mouth, pull out the triangles as shown, then fold in half.

11 Tuck in the edges.

12 To make the mouth speak, hold the model at the points shown, then gently move your hands together and apart.

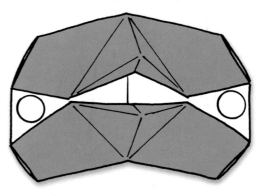

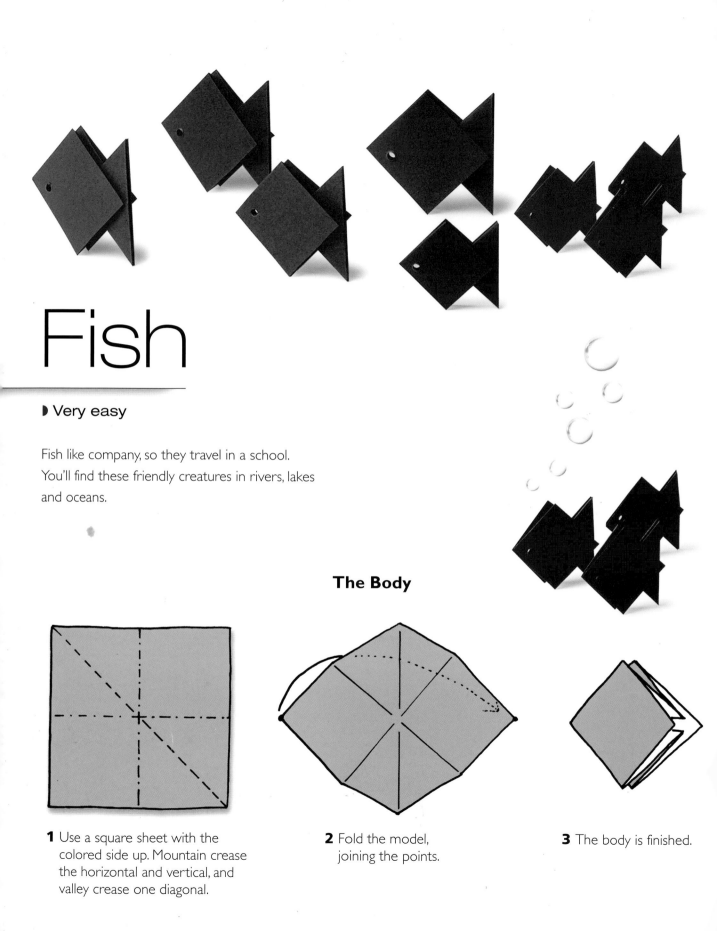

Fish

▶ **Very easy**

Fish like company, so they travel in a school.
You'll find these friendly creatures in rivers, lakes
and oceans.

The Body

1 Use a square sheet with the colored side up. Mountain crease the horizontal and vertical, and valley crease one diagonal.

2 Fold the model, joining the points.

3 The body is finished.

The Tail

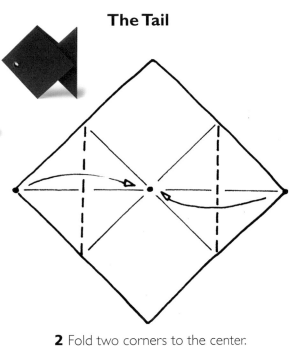

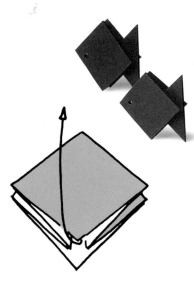

1 Make the same model as the body, then unfold.

2 Fold two corners to the center.

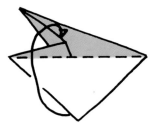

3 Fold and unfold the other two corners to the center.

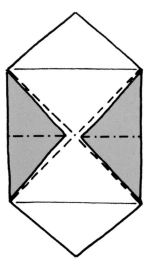

4 Refold the unit as in step 1, bringing in the two triangles.

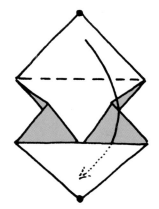

5 Fold the rear triangle inside to lock the layers.

6 Fold the front triangle inside, the same way.

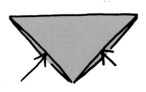

7 The unit has two pockets for assembly.

Assembly

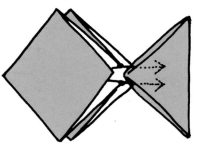

1 Slide the inside points of the body into the pockets of the tail.

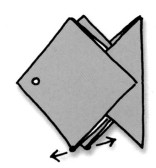

2 For the fish to stand, gently separate the points. Draw an eye with a pencil or punch a hole in the paper.

Rabbit

▶ **Very easy**

This naughty rabbit is nibbling on the carrots in my garden. With his ears up he stays on guard, ready to bolt at the slightest noise.

1 Crease the center of a square of paper.

2 Fold the edges along the center crease.

3 Fold up the triangle.

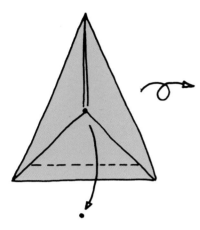

4 Make a pleat fold by bringing the triangle down. Then turn it over.

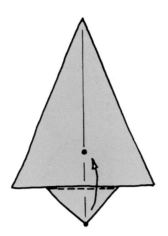

5 To make the tail, fold up the triangle.

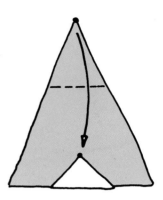

6 To make the head, fold the point toward the bottom.

Enlarged view

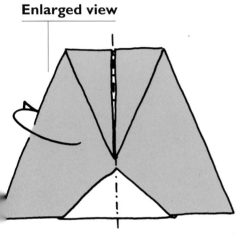

7 Fold in half.

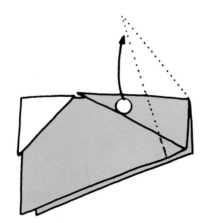

8 Bring up the points of the ears.

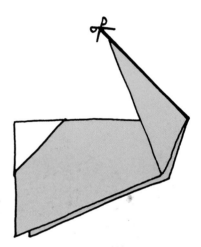

9 Separate the ears by cutting them.

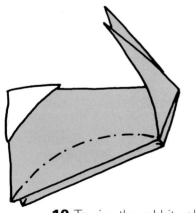

10 To give the rabbit volume, curve the sides with your thumbs.

11 The last fold gives a sense of movement to the rabbit.

Envelope

▶ Very easy

This envelope is a very practical creation. Use it to hold pictures, stamps and all your other little treasures.

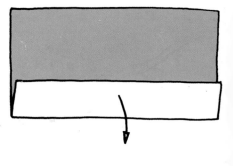

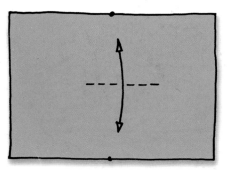

1 Partially crease the center of an A4 sheet (see page 6).

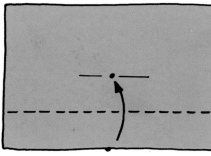

2 Fold the bottom edge to the center crease …

3 … then unfold.

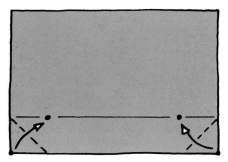

4 Fold the two corners up along the crease.

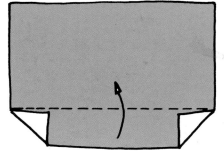

5 Fold the bottom strip back up …

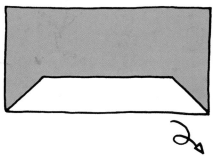

6 … Like this, then turn it over.

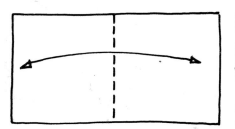

7 Crease the center.

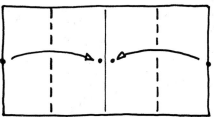

8 Fold the sides along the center crease.

Enlarged view

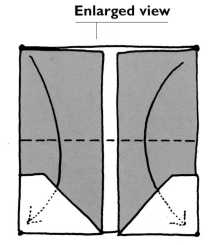

9 Fold in half, sliding corners into the pockets.

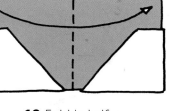

10 Fold in half.

11 The envelope has two outside pockets and …

12 … two inside pockets, as well as a large pocket when it is opened underneath.

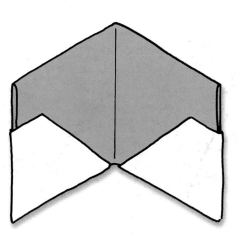

Airplane

▶ **Very easy**

All passengers please proceed to the check-in counter for immediate boarding. This little airplane will fly better if launched in the direction of the wind. Have a good flight!

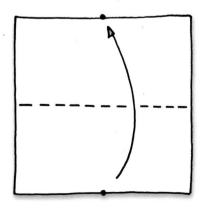

1 Fold a square of paper in half.

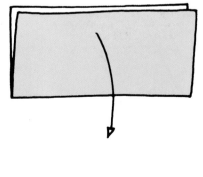

2 Unfold.

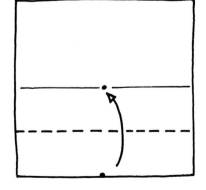

3 Fold up the lower edge along the center crease.

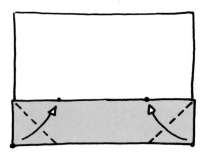

4 Fold the two lower corners.

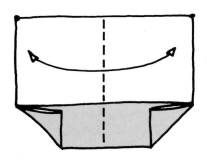

5 Crease the center.

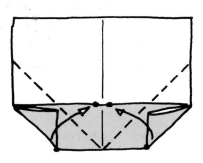

6 Fold up the edges along the center crease.

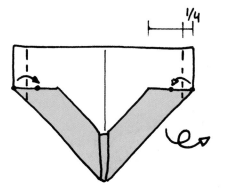

7 Fold the ailerons as shown, then turn the model over.

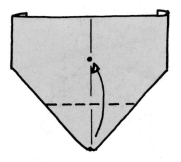

8 Fold up the point.

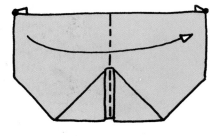

9 Fold in half.

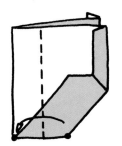

10 Fold one wing by joining the points …

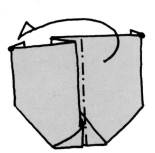

11 … then the other wing.

12 To increase the stability of the plane, fold the wings back up to horizontal and adjust the ailerons (see step 7).

Boat

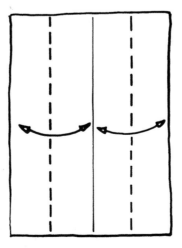

▶ **Very easy**

Decorate your boat, give it a name
and then launch it in your bathtub.

1 Crease the center of a
half-A4 sheet (see page 6
and page 14).

2 Crease the edges along
the center.

3 Fold the three corners
shown.

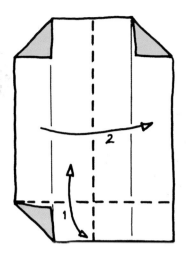

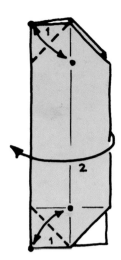

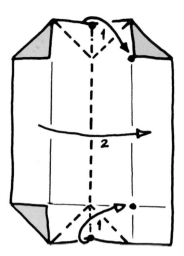

4 Crease horizontally (1) along the lower corner, then fold in half (2).

5 Crease the upper and lower corners (1), then unfold (2).

6 Pull the triangles, top and bottom (1), into inside reverse folds (see page 9) by refolding in half (2).

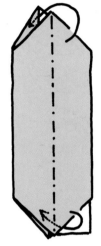

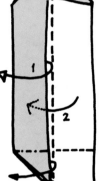

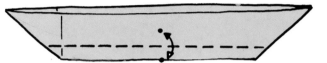

9 With the model flat, crease one third with a valley crease, then a mountain crease (see page 6).

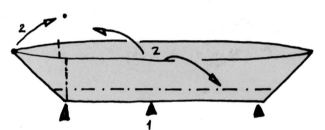

7 To lock the ends, fold the strip inside and under the different layers at both ends.

8 Open gently (1) and fold the other strip inside (2).

10 To shape the bottom of the boat, push on the lower strip (1) by clearly marking the mountain crease. Then give the boat volume by folding up the back (2).

Enlarged view

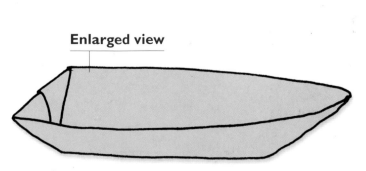

11 Fold the upper triangle (1) inside; then fold the small triangle (2) at the bottom, under.

12 This flat-bottomed boat floats very well.

Simple Stars

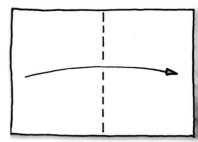

A snip of the scissors, a few folds … and then, like magic, a galaxy of stars will appear in different sizes and styles.

1 Fold an A4 or A5 sheet (see page 6 and page 14) in half.

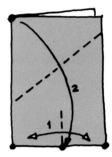

2 Mark the midpoint of the lower edge (1), then fold down the upper-left corner (2) to the middle of the side.

Enlarged view

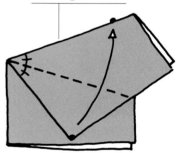

3 Fold the flap up along the upper edge.

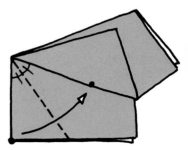

4 Fold the left side to the folded edge.

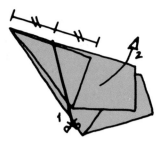

5 Fold in half toward the back.

6a Cut through all layers carefully (1), then unfold the point (2).

6b Give the star volume by making valley and mountain creases (see page 6) as shown.

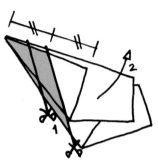

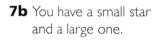

7a Cut along two parallel lines (1), then unfold the pieces (2).

7b You have a small star and a large one.

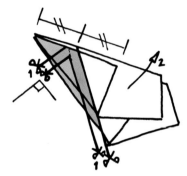

8a Cut as shown (1), taking note of the right angle, then unfold the small piece (2).

8b You have another type of star.

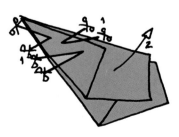

9a Cut out notches on the two sides (1), then unfold the sheet (2).

9b You have a star in the center of the sheet.

Decorations

▶▶ Easy

Just change the number of cuts and their locations to create different styles of stars. Stick these decorations on a window and admire their beauty in the light.

The Star

Enlarged view

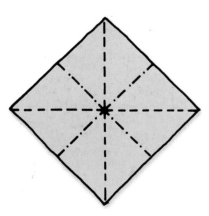

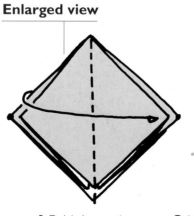

1 Start with a preliminary base (see page 7).

4 Fold the entire model in half.

3 Make a crease by folding an edge over along the vertical edge (1), then cut along the crease through all layers (2).

4 Make three parallel cuts, then unfold the whole thing.

5 Fold the four small triangles toward the center.

6 Slide the four largest triangles under the first set.

7 Make all the valley and mountain creases as shown.

The Square

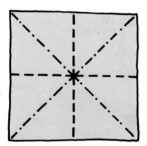

1 Start with a waterbomb base (see page 8).

Enlarged view

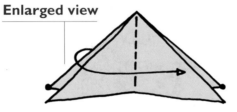

2 Fold the entire model in half.

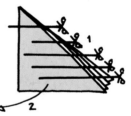

3 Make parallel cuts (1), stopping at different distances from the vertical edge. Unfold the model (2).

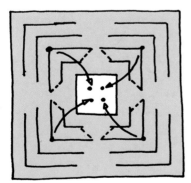

4 Fold the first four points toward the center.

5 Fold the points near the edge under the first set.

6 To flatten well, place under a pile of heavy books for several days.

Box and House

Easy

Only a tiny person could live in this delightful little house. But with just two folds and a spin, the house becomes a box ... perfect for candy.

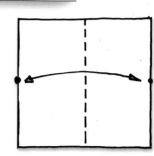

1 Crease the center of a square.

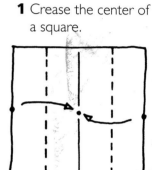

2 Fold the sides along the center crease ...

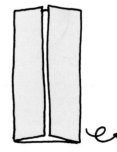
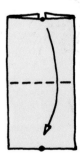

3 ... like this, then turn it over.

4 Fold in half.

Enlarged view

5 Crease the corners by joining the points.

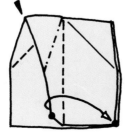

6 To make the corner a reverse fold, fold one layer to the right, pushing in the corner ...

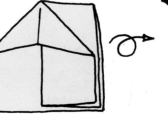

7 ... like this, then turn it over.

8 Fold the other corner the same way.

9 Flip the upper layer in front to the left and the rear one to the right.

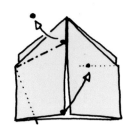

10 Bring the lower corner up to the dotted horizontal line …

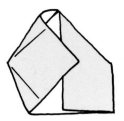

11 … then flatten.

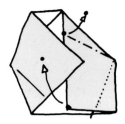

12 Repeat steps 10 and 11 on the other corner …

Enlarged view

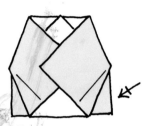

13 … like this. Repeat the steps on the two corners on the other side.

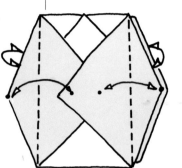

14 Crease the sides front and back.

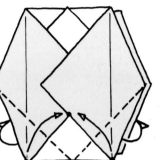

15 Fold up the lower triangles by joining the points. Repeat behind.

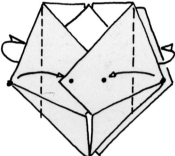

16 Refold the sides. Repeat behind..

The House

The Box

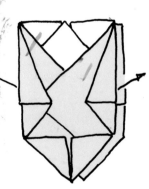

17 Give the house volume by placing your fingers inside and sharpening the creases.

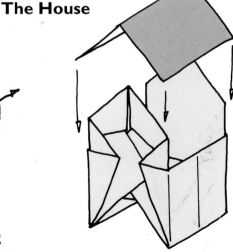

18 To make the roof, simply fold a small square or rectangle in half.

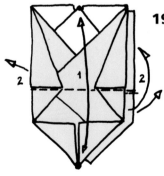

19 After step 16, crease as shown on both sides (1), then give the box shape by putting your fingers inside (2).

20 To make nesting boxes (boxes that fit inside one another) just fold them from slightly smaller squares.

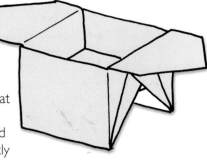

Bracelet

Decorate these beautiful colored bracelets to suit your taste or give them to your friends. If you use longer and wider strips, you can make a headband or decorative belt.

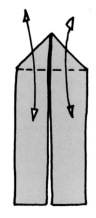

1 Cut a strip of paper from an A4 sheet (see page 14). For a bracelet with three motifs, cut a strip 1 in./2 cm wide; for a bracelet with five motifs, cut a strip ⅝ in./1.5 cm wide.

2 Crease the middle.

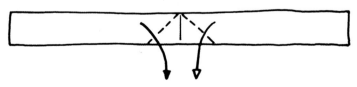

3 Fold the strip down along the center crease on both sides.

4 Make the horizontal crease by folding up both ends of the strip.

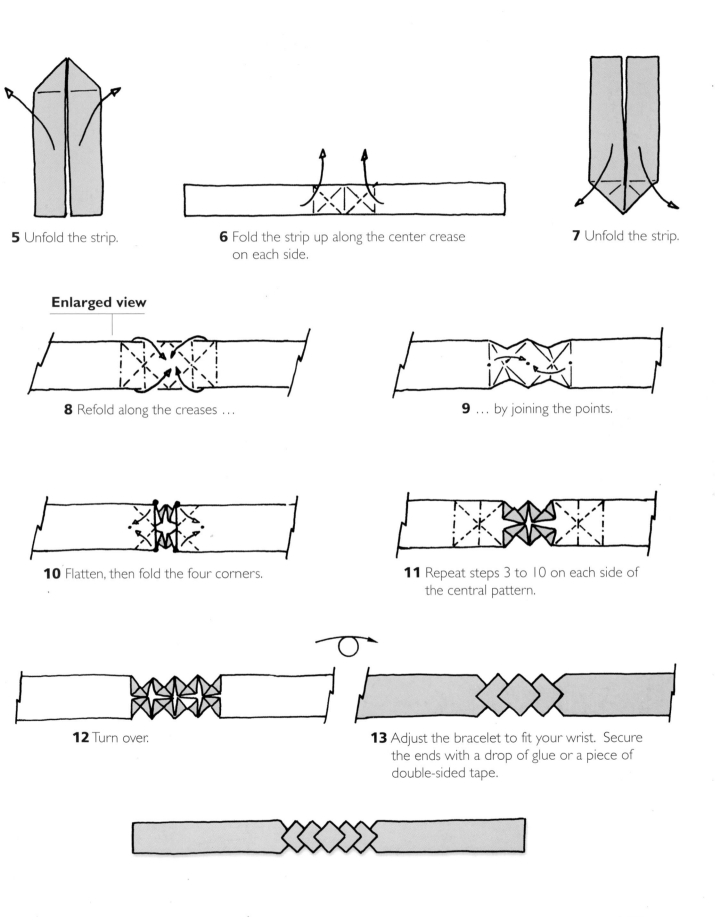

5 Unfold the strip.

6 Fold the strip up along the center crease on each side.

7 Unfold the strip.

Enlarged view

8 Refold along the creases …

9 … by joining the points.

10 Flatten, then fold the four corners.

11 Repeat steps 3 to 10 on each side of the central pattern.

12 Turn over.

13 Adjust the bracelet to fit your wrist. Secure the ends with a drop of glue or a piece of double-sided tape.

Propeller

▶▶ Easy

A little quick folding and the propeller is ready to turn with the slightest breeze. Use bright colors and watch how they mix when the propeller spins.

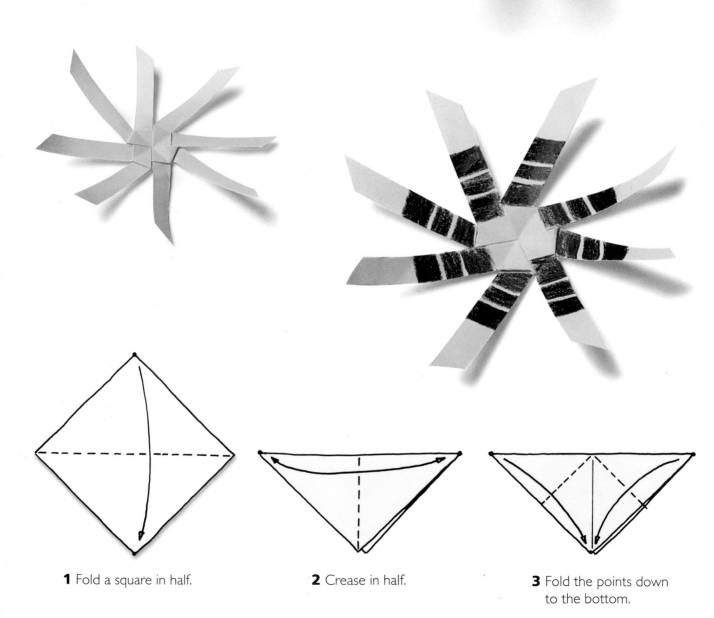

1 Fold a square in half.

2 Crease in half.

3 Fold the points down to the bottom.

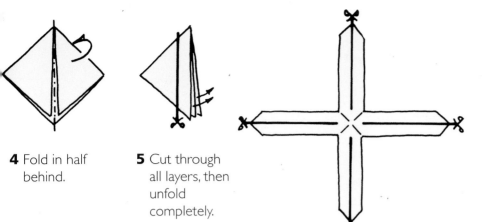

4 Fold in half behind.

5 Cut through all layers, then unfold completely.

6 Split each strip by cutting.

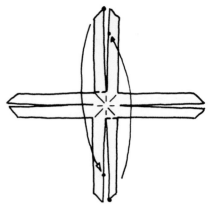

7 Bring down the top left strip and bring up the bottom right strip.

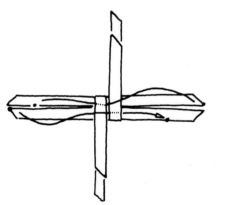

8 Pass one strip over and under from the right and one from the left …

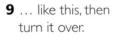

9 … like this, then turn it over.

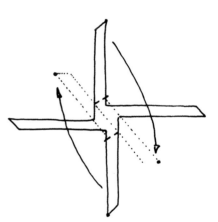

10 Fold the upper and lower strips at an angle.

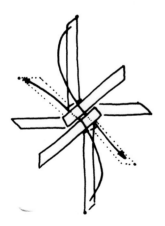

11 Weave the last two strips.

12 Twist the ends, then make valley creases in the center to raise the arms of the propeller.

13 There are several ways to make the propeller spin. Place it on a table and blow on it gently; hold it level and let it drop; or attach it to a taut thread.

Face

▶▶ Easy

A pointed nose or a round one? Blue eyes or brown eyes? Mouth open or closed? It's your choice when you make these funny faces.

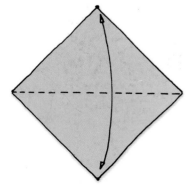

1 Crease a square in half.

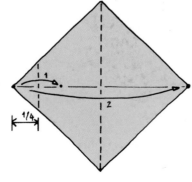

2 Fold in the corner one-quarter of the way (1), then fold in half (2).

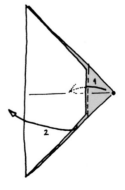

3 Fold the exposed corner to the inside to match the first corner folded (1), then open the model (2).

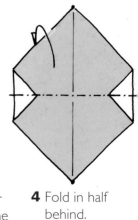

4 Fold in half behind.

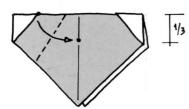

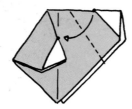

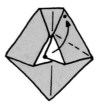

5 Fold the left corner in thirds, then join the points.

6 Fold the other corner the same way.

7 Bring up the right side as shown.

Enlarged view

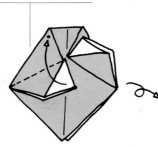

8 Fold up the left side, then turn over.

Enlarged view

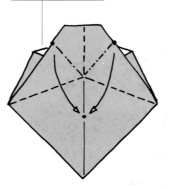

9 Fold down the sides along two corresponding valley folds on the other side and flatten.

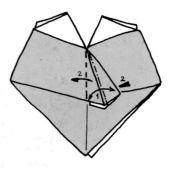

10 To give shape to the nose, crease along the upper layer (1), then spread open and flatten (2).

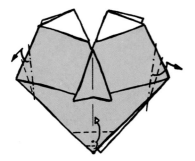

11 Make pleat folds for the ears. For the mouth, fold the point up, then fold again.

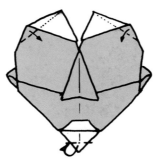

12 To finish the mouth, fold the point behind, then shape the eyes by folding forward, as shown.

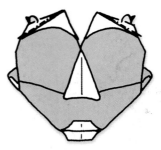

13 Fold back the part behind the eyes.

String of Dolls

▶▶▶ More challenging

Make some simple folds and scissor cuts, and you have a string of little dancing people. To make a circle, join several strings together.

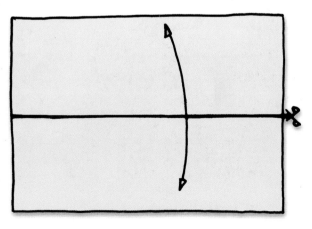

1 Fold an A4 sheet in half, then cut along the crease.

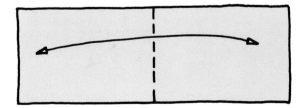

2 Crease the center.

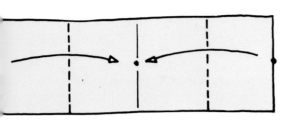  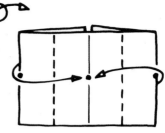

3 Fold the edges along the center crease …

4 … like this, then turn it over.

5 Fold the sides to the center crease, freeing the layers behind.

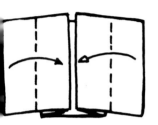

6 Fold in the remaining strips the same way.

Enlarged view

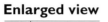 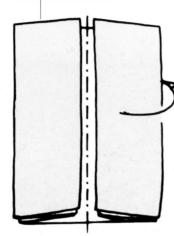

7 Fold in half behind.

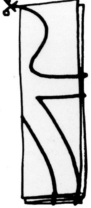

8 With a pencil, draw the silhouette of a person, then cut through all layers.

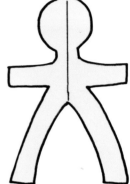

9 Unfold completely to show the string.

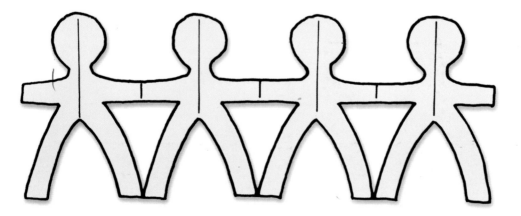

10 To make a circle of dolls, make another string with the leftover half and glue the ends together.

Cube

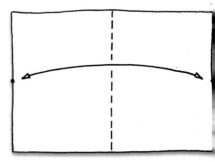

▶▶▶ More challenging

This model is made with six different colored pieces of paper. You can attach several cubes together with the help of straws or rods, either inserted right through the cube or along the edges.

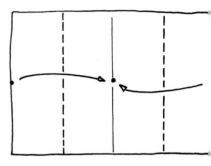

1 Start with an A4 or A6 sheet (see page 14). Crease the center.

2 Fold the edges to the center crease.

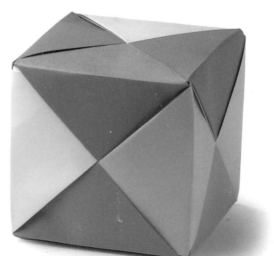

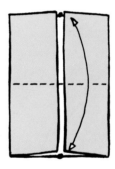

3 Crease the center.

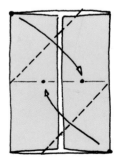

4 Fold the corners along the center crease …

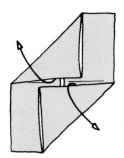

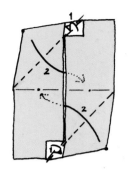

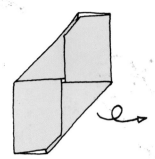

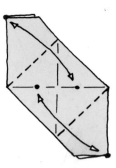

5 … like this, then unfold the corners.

6 Fold the small corners inside (1), then slide the two corners between the two layers (2) …

7 … like this, then turn it over.

8 Make two creases by joining the points. This creates the assembly tabs. Make five more units in the same way.

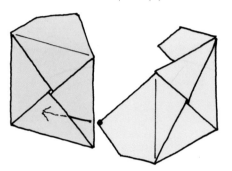

9 Slide the tab of the first unit between the layers of the second unit.

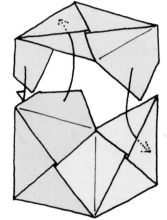

10 Slide in the two tabs of the third unit like the previous ones, then rotate the model.

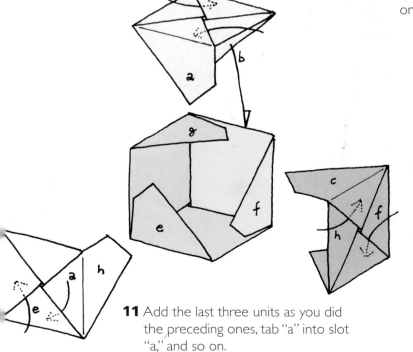

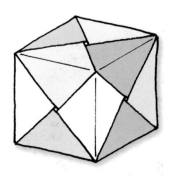

11 Add the last three units as you did the preceding ones, tab "a" into slot "a," and so on.

12 Have fun making cubes of different sizes.

Fancy Star and Ball

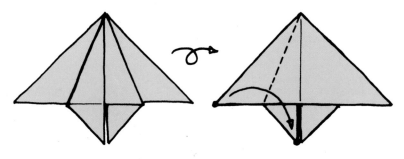

▶▶▶ More challenging

This star needs just a bit of patience and a little attention to detail to make a beautiful creation.

The Star

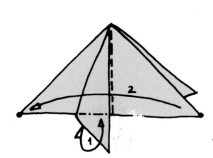

1 First make a cube (see page 50) from A5 paper. Set aside for now. From a 7 in./18 cm square, fold a waterbomb base (see page 8), then fold down one side along the center crease.

2 Mountain crease the lower point (1), then fold one layer to the left (2).

3 Fold the second side like the first.

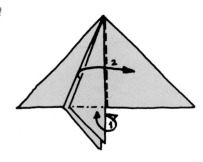

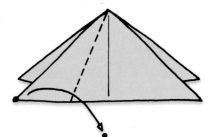

4 Mountain crease the lower point (1), then fold the layer back to the right (2) …

5 … like this, then turn it over.

6 Repeat the same operation for the third layer.

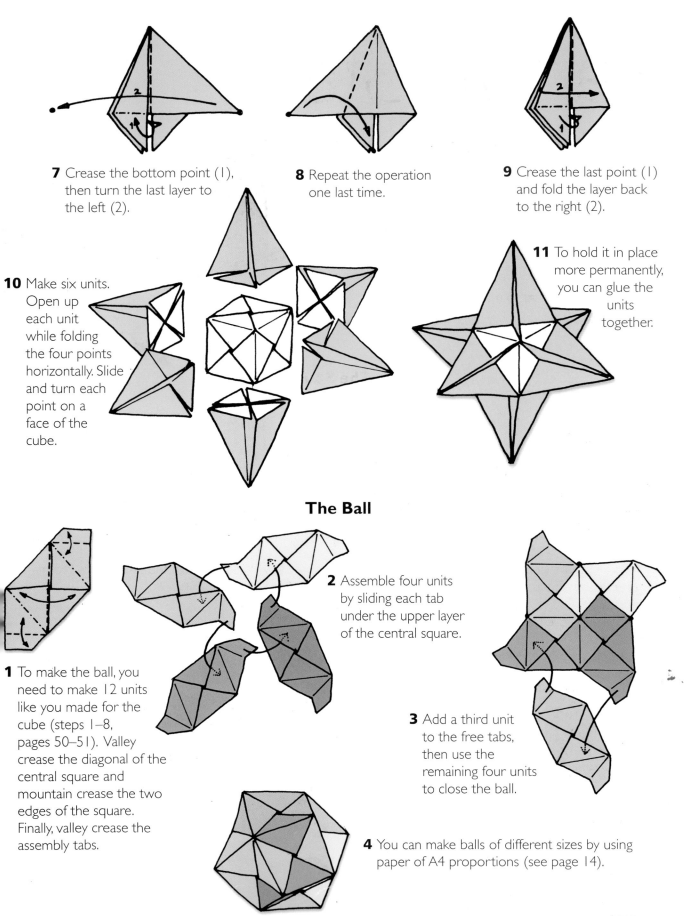

7 Crease the bottom point (1), then turn the last layer to the left (2).

8 Repeat the operation one last time.

9 Crease the last point (1) and fold the layer back to the right (2).

10 Make six units. Open up each unit while folding the four points horizontally. Slide and turn each point on a face of the cube.

11 To hold it in place more permanently, you can glue the units together.

The Ball

1 To make the ball, you need to make 12 units like you made for the cube (steps 1–8, pages 50–51). Valley crease the diagonal of the central square and mountain crease the two edges of the square. Finally, valley crease the assembly tabs.

2 Assemble four units by sliding each tab under the upper layer of the central square.

3 Add a third unit to the free tabs, then use the remaining four units to close the ball.

4 You can make balls of different sizes by using paper of A4 proportions (see page 14).

Star Cluster

)))) More challenging

Starting with this basic module, you can create a series of stars, each more complex in design, to decorate your room or a holiday table.

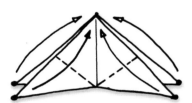

The Star

Enlarged view

1 Start with a waterbomb base (see page 8), then fold the points up front and back.

2 Fold the four points down.

3 Unfold completely, then push in the center to change the direction of the folds.

4 Fold along the creases to make a preliminary base (see page 7).

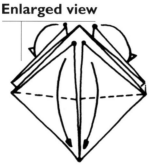

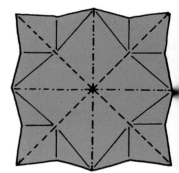

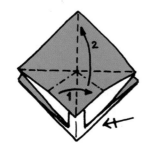

5 Pinch the point in half by creasing as shown (1), then bring up the flap (2). Repeat this step on the other side.

6 Fold one flap to the right, then on the back fold one flap to the left. Repeat step 5 for the other two faces.

7 The star will be completed once it is joined to the base.

The Base

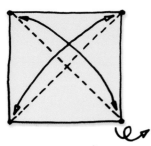

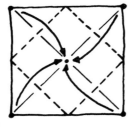

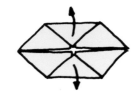

1 Start with a square the same size as used for the star. Crease the diagonals by joining the points, then turn it over.

2 Fold the corners to the center.

3 Fold in the upper and lower corners.

4 Unfold the two corners.

5 Open while refolding the points to the center.

Enlarged view

6 Bring the four triangles to the vertical folds.

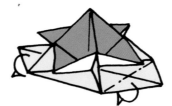

Assembly

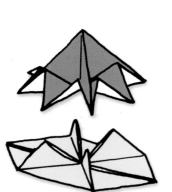

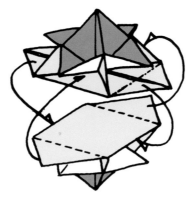

1 Slide each of the four points of the star into the triangles of the base. To make the assembly easier, you can partially unfold the base.

2 Mountain fold the sides.

3 This star with its base can be used to decorate a holiday table.

4 You can also cross two units back to back, then fold the sides into each other to close the model. By assembling six units in the same way, into a cube, you can make the large star cluster on page 54.

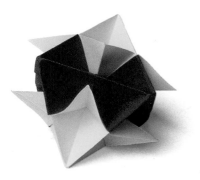

What's This?

What is this? Is it an observatory? A space vessel? You decide. Use your imagination.

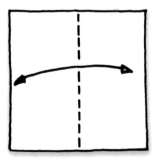

1 Start with a square the same size used for the star (page 54). Crease the center.

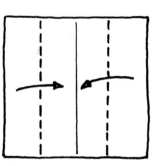

2 Fold the sides.

3 Fold in the four corners.

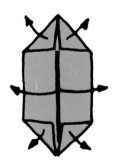

4 Unfold completely.

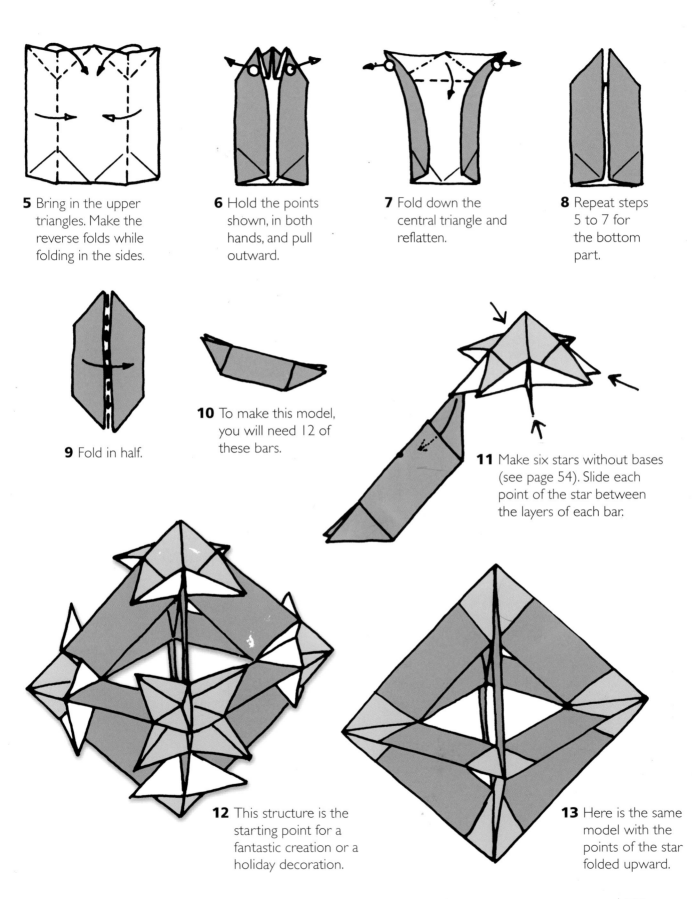

5 Bring in the upper triangles. Make the reverse folds while folding in the sides.

6 Hold the points shown, in both hands, and pull outward.

7 Fold down the central triangle and reflatten.

8 Repeat steps 5 to 7 for the bottom part.

9 Fold in half.

10 To make this model, you will need 12 of these bars.

11 Make six stars without bases (see page 54). Slide each point of the star between the layers of each bar.

12 This structure is the starting point for a fantastic creation or a holiday decoration.

13 Here is the same model with the points of the star folded upward.

Garland

You can decorate the house for the holidays with these multicolored garlands. Make lots and lots of small ones and string them together like pearls on a length of strong thread.

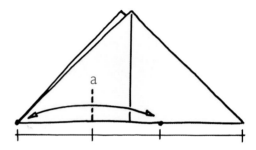

1 Crease a square sheet vertically (1), then fold up in half (2).

2 To divide perfectly in thirds, crease approximately one-third (a).

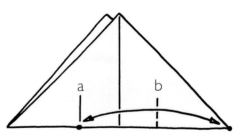

3 Make a second crease (b) by joining the points.

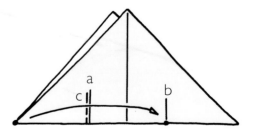

4 Make a third crease (c) by joining the points.

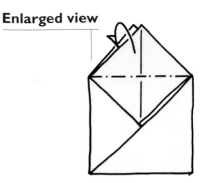

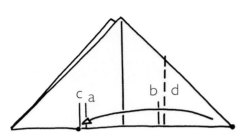

5 Finally, fold the right point to join (c).

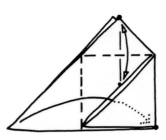

6 Fold the other side inside the first, then crease the upper triangle through one layer.

7 Open the top slightly and tuck the upper triangle inside.

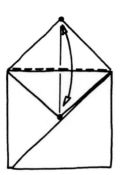

8 Crease the other triangle.

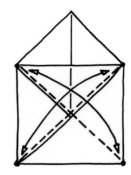

9 Crease the diagonals with a mountain crease and a valley crease.

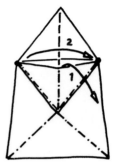

10 Open the shape by pinching the small (1) and large triangles (2).

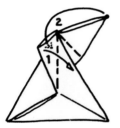

11 To close the model, fold the small triangle (1) to the side, then tuck the point of the large triangle (2) inside the small one.

12 Make a set of small units in several colors, then …

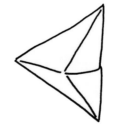

13 … using thread and a long needle, string the units together one by one, alternating colors.

Pyramid

▶▶▶ **More challenging**

The pyramids of Egypt were filled with rich treasures. These little pyramids can serve as money boxes or banks. Slide your money in along the edges; take it out by lifting the little pointed top.

The Base

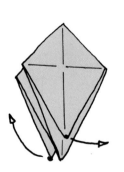

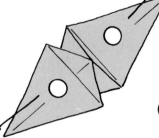

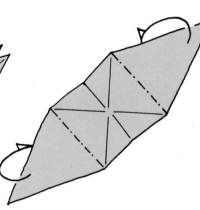

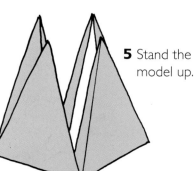

1 Start with a bird base (see page 10), then fold the two points down.

2 Pull the two points out at the same time, halfway.

3 Hold the points shown, in both hands, then pull lightly to make the square bottom of the pyramid.

4 Join the four points.

5 Stand the model up.

The Top

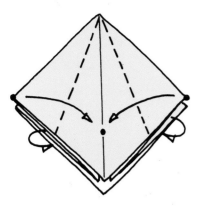

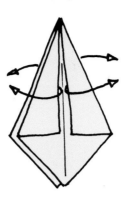

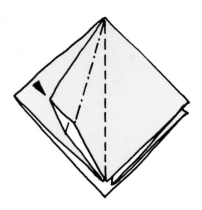

1 Start with a preliminary base (see page 7) made with a smaller square, then fold the edges along the center crease on both faces.

2 Unfold the sides.

3 Raise one side to vertical, then open as you flatten it.

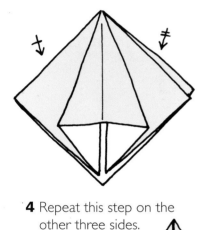

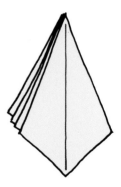

4 Repeat this step on the other three sides.

5 Fold the front layer to the right, then fold the back layer to the left.

6 Give it shape by making four faces.

Assembly

1 Put the inner folds of the top between the edges of the pyramid.

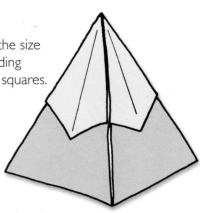

2 You can change the size of the top by folding smaller or larger squares.

Bird

▶▶ **More challenging**

When spring arrives, these birds will want to sing and show off their magnificent plumage. Find the birds a home on a table or in your room.

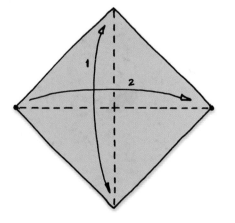

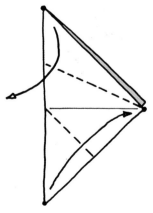

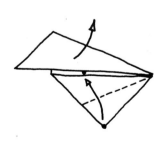

1 Crease a large square horizontally (1), then fold in half to the right (2).

2 Fold the upper edge along the center crease, then fold the lower edge in half by joining the points.

3 Unfold the upper part, then fold the lower triangle in half along the center crease.

4 Unfold completely

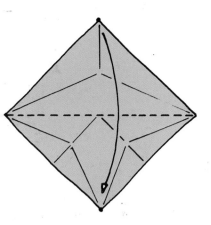

5 Fold in half to the bottom.

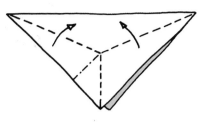

6 Fold the top layer, bringing the sides up at the same time to make a rabbit ear fold (see page 11).

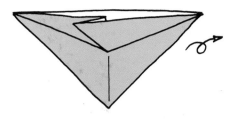

7 Flatten, then turn over.

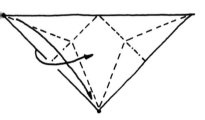

8 Bring the sides into reverse folds …

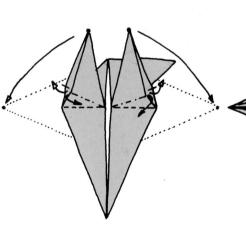

9 … and join the points at the bottom.

Enlarged view

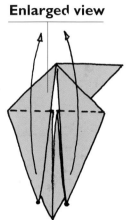

10 Make a horizontal fold by bringing up the points.

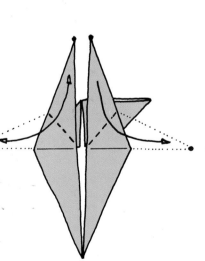

11 To crease the legs, crease the points to each side as shown by dotted lines.

12 Open each point and fold flat to each side.

Leg details

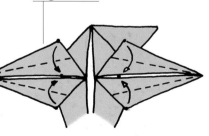

13a To refine the legs, fold in the edges, leaving a space in the center.

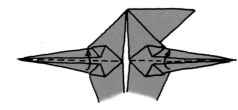

13b Refold the points in half, upward.

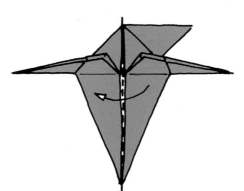

14 Fold the model in half.

15 To make the body, crease the point on the right as far as the dotted lines, then make an outside reverse fold by opening the point slightly (see page 9).

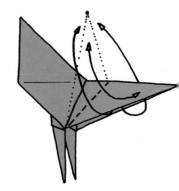

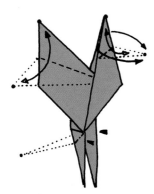

16 To make the tail, crease the left point by folding as far as the dotted lines. For the head, crease as shown, then make an outside reverse fold. For the legs, crease and then make an inside reverse fold (see page 9).

17 Open the upper point of the tail and then flatten it to each side. For the head, release some paper from inside and flatten. Crease the legs, then make an inside reverse fold.

Feet details

18a Crease, then open the point.

18b Mountain crease the upper edges of the triangle, then bring up the point.

18c Swivel the point forward along the folds of the triangles while folding the leg in half.

Head details

19a Fold the point.

19b Fold the point back, then unfold.

19c Make a pleat fold while opening the point.

View of face

20 Round out the body of the bird. To make it stand, hold it by the legs with one hand and adjust the body slightly forward or back with the other.